Notebook

While every precaution has been taken in the preparation of this book, the publisher assumes no responsibility for errors or omissions, or for damages resulting from the use of the information contained herein.

NOTEBOOK

First edition. July 14, 2024.

ISBN: 979-8227107251

Written by T.Charles Rampedi.

All the names were changed to protect one's identity

I don't know if I'm supposed to be greeting you or what, nor am I valid enough to know what I'm going to write inside here. Maybe my notes or lyrics I don't know, but what I can say is that these days I lost all feelings to the hobbies that made me happy, I'm just numb now. But I think I'll start writing my thoughts in this book because there's nothing much going on in my life. Still lonely but sometimes I feel happy that I am, sometimes not. So, my thoughts for today seem to be blank, but one thing that I can tell you is that I'm not happy nor joyfully sad, and it's technically not boredom, trust me I can do better by myself, there's no need to get bored when you are me. But yah, daily thoughts will be written or stated when things turn to be sideways.

Before I go further, I guess I must introduce myself since this is the first of... I don't know how many will be there, but this is my first. The name is Dimpho, male, currently 20 years of age. Believe it, a guy in his 20s writing in a journal, or as some may call it, "Dear Diary" is weird.

Technically it is but honestly writing helps me explain or communicate more than I usually can verbally do so. I express myself through writing, that's why I got into music, poetry and some art and crafty things which girls find weird, cause guys don't do that. But I really don't, like I said, I don't find those hobbies of rapping, writing poems, drawing etc., very interesting, and it's not because I'm maturing or whatever it may be called.

So, I'm the lonely creepy guy in the stories or movies that everybody hates up until the end, when that person is gone, and they realize that the reasons why he did these things are sad. Okay I'm not that creepy I think, but yah, I'm lonely, I've got no friends, my social media platforms where I'm supposed to make friends are filled with people, but I talk to none cause unfortunately, I'm "boring" or "not interesting", words used by them. Thats why I don't play much on social media, I was also told to go out more, socialize physically so, in person, but I'm not a fan of crowded places, I prefer silence, peace and fresh air instead of pubs, clubs, and events.

It's not my fault because believe me I tried to change or tried to step in the lane of being a normal human being, but like they said in high school I'm an alien. The thing about calling myself creepy, I don't call myself that, but I'm classified as a creep according to the people, it's because I can't talk to a person without knowing that person. In other words I can or I am able to read peoples personalities, like the type of person you are, what offends you, what are your insecurities and etc. by just analyzing you I can read you, and it's not a thing whereby I had to read a book written by the greatest minds, NO, it's just something that occurred naturally.

Unfortunately, it's not something that I want but I have no option in having it or not. Maybe that's because I grew up alone instead of filling my head with hide-and-seek games, no offence. Guess what? Again, based on the internet I'm an overthinker, and it's not like I'm just saying these things because I like them or maybe I want to be them. My personality, to me is unexplainable, but the things that I do relate to what they are saying, it's like bumping into an article on the internet and you turn to read it just to find out that that article is talking about you. For me sometimes when I find those stuff I turn to tear or tears start dropping from my face, not because I'm weird, I don't cry, I'm not a crybaby, I am a MAN. But it's just weird when you bump into something, and it perfectly describes you with all the small details in it. If you're like me and have no one who knows you like that, and you bump into that, it's awesome.

So, to sum me up, this is me, the ugly, low self-esteem, weird, overthinker, lonely, a little bit stupid, depressed guy with dreams only to rely on to enjoy life, unable to communicate with strangers.

I believe that's me, but not to overlook some of the things, the two people who I'm currently talking to at the moment are Memo who is a friend, but we partially talk much, cause she's got friends of her own, as a girl and SpongeBob my situationship for the past three years, yes I had to point that out I guess. While still on that note of the things that end up with -tionship, my past relationships weren't actually a success. I like identifying them as a moment of friendship, even though me and those people were dating. I haven't been in a relationship in the past five years ago, and before those certain years I dated only three girls. In my life, I only dated them, and they all broke up with me cause unfortunately, I wasn't able to say those three magical words to their face nor even be able to express my feelings through talking.

Before you get mad, or say I'm like every guy, and use that bad language you're thinking of in your head, no, I did not date them all at once. You start dating one person, they break you and you move on. It was like that.

So I got heartbroken, by the first for that reason, and again with the second but with the third it was because I wasn't famous enough with the hole making music thing, and I know that cause she broke up with me for a certain guy who does music and he's actually well known, was at the time, I don't know about now. I don't feel bad honestly, nor feel like saying they'll regret or feel hatred for them, cause during those past two I was dealing with somethings and music was my escape, like it was hard for me and it's still hard for me to even say that I love you to someone. So, I never said it out loud to them, but I could text it, nor even did I feel comfortable being around them because I never allowed them to kiss me nor I to them.

Just to point out this again, I didn't date them simultaneously so. I've tried to date other girls over the past 5 years, but unfortunately, rejection became my so-called friend, and unfortunately, I didn't know why I wasn't their type. But I can't blame them to be real, I'm nobody's type to be exact. But I found hope in a girl called SpongeBob, but today or let me just say I fell deeply in love with her, and she never felt the same way, but the dopamine, serotonin and oxytocin kept feeding me stupid ideas such as;

Never give up, "she likes you" and "she can't stop thinking about you" which was stupid. Consistency in the title of love or searching made me look stupid, that's why I don't think of it.

Today it all just went south, or I took it south to be more specific I guess after reading that message she showed me of her boyfriend. I just kind of broke to pieces. Thats why I just said we could be friends, and unfortunately, I don't know how to keep friends, trust me.

The only reason why I said OKAY to that is because everyone who ends up being my friend eventually stops talking to me as life goes on. So, I guess I'm also hoping for the same thing. I'm supposed to be happy, because she broke my heart, and that was what I was hoping for or fall in love but, I got the results, but I'm feeling numb like, why can't I feel the pain in my heart, do you have a clue?

I need to cry but I can't cry without the pain, so I'm just laying here on my bed writing here with no emotions.

Okay, if these are the results of getting heartbroken multiple times it's fine, I managed to do it, but am I proud now, because I don't know. But like, I feel nothing now. Maybe it will be different as time goes on but for now, I just remain clueless whatsoever, which led me to draw the conclusion which states that I'm not supposed to fall in love, love is not for me.

No matter how much I try to find it, I'm supposed to grow old alone, by myself. Sometimes I like to think that I'm the lucky one, because I prefer being by myself sometimes, and it's not optional, cause most of the time I just get ignored or I'm not wanted by people around them.

Sometimes bad things are said which literally I don't care about, but I turn to care a lot when those people pretend to me. It's painful, I guess, that's why I came up with this theory about love to help me feel better, but it only works partially now. But most of the time it doesn't work at all.

I told myself that the only reason why people date each other or have friends is because they are lonely, and they are afraid of being or feeling that little moment of loneliness. Thats why our parents told us to make friends when we were young. That's why Eve was created in the garden of Eden; it's reasonable, but it sometimes doesn't work. I'm in love with the pain, and it's stupid and uncalled for, because I want to be unique, not like everybody in this world, but it doesn't mean I must be sad and miserable. But unfortunately, nobody can tell right, because I've spent countless years perfecting my smile so that nobody could tell if I'm feeling a certain way.

My heart feels like its eating itself most of the time and I wish I could stop it honestly, I wish I could, but I can't, the only thing that's spinning in my mind now it's to say <u>the broken is better than the fixed, because nobody will use you recklessly however they wish without knowing your value, for a bruise will always be left to them, if they do</u>. Sometimes I have the urge, like I wish I could talk to people because I envy what they have, but I'm me right, all fucked up. So, if I may ask you as you're reading this, what's love according to you? Is it the sex, how pretty your boyfriend or girlfriend looks so you can brag about him or her?

Do tell.

Cause I technically thought it was all about caring, cause caring leads to love, love leads to something which nobody can describe. But no matter how much I express my feelings or start caring about someone because I like that person whom I care about, it's not like that.

So, what's the point of dating, do tell me...?

I know that girls can be snakes, but I never thought all of them could be like that honestly. So why should I get married, why should I be in love if all that's going to happen is to be led on like a kid following cookie crumps taking me to a path that ends in the middle of nowhere. Lost, nowhere to be found, nor unrecognized in the place I was led to. What's the point of having kids, but this one I don't mind, raising kids is amazing, but let's continue, what's the point of being in a relationship cause I'm never going to be the first choice in other people's eyes, nor the second or third, nor fourth or fifth.

I'm the person who everybody turns to when they've got no other alternatives or any other options ahead. All the girls that I've tried dating are always saying they prefer us if we could just be friends, that's one of the reasons why it will feel like what I wrote in here doesn't make sense. So, what's the point of falling exactly, because I know that I'm just going to crash-land, right, so I'm just going to focus on building my career, I guess.

Like I always dreamt right, but, what if something happens as well, like the whole thing of building my name like the famous Charles Richter, Charles Darwin and others, combust into pieces to ashes. I know I was born as nothing but sometimes I feel like I can't go out without the whole world not knowing me, cause those who know me, know me as pathetic, useless, weird, idiot and the list just keeps going on.

So, I guess I'll focus on that, you know. Thinking about myself when I was young, saying that I'm going to grow up, have a girlfriend whose going to love me like damn, saying that I'm going to have the best friend in the world, a friend whose going to be there through thick and thin, those buddies who do sleepovers, trade shirts, and all those types of things best friends do.

Well, I wish I could design a time machine and go back and tell that guy no such thing is going to happen, everything is going to change in the future, better buckle up. Cause all those are just dreams, and most dreams don't come true. That you're going to battle a lot of monsters like darkness, loneliness and some I can't mention here, and you're going to get hurt, bruised, mentally and physically to a point where you're going to write your mother a letter to say goodbye but never have the gut to pull it through, the only way to fix your problems it's to design a perfect fake smile which nobody could recognize not even your own parents, become an idiot and a joker about everything so they could think that you're the happiest person in this world, while at night, when your alone listening to sad music that talks to you and the only way for you to talk back is by crying, and start avoiding people because being around them makes you sad as they show real happy smiles while yours is fake.

I wish I could tell you to stop dreaming, cause a tsunami of sadness and depression is coming to drown you and no matter what you do, any reason you come up with it's not going to make sense for you, but it's going to deepen you into that dark hallow void in your heart. Dreaming is good, it's going to be awesome once you get the hang of it, but people are going to call you crazy, mentally disturb and other offending things, because you going to do it all the time. Think about funny movie parts you watched, start smiling or giggling alone, think about things that make you happy like cartoons, jokes and all that, but you're going to let them go. I don't know why, but it's not because of the bad comments people are going to give you but, your thoughts are going to need you to feed them, erase your dreams.

So, guess what I'm doing right now, I call my dreams, illusions, cause that's all they are right. I can't rely on my memories when I was a kid cause during that time, I was dreaming about how happy I'm going to be in my teenage days, my teenage days are over and what I dreamt about hasn't happen.

I can't dream about the future too, because it's going to be the same, so now I'm just living this boring sad life of my own ink. Let me guess reader, you are going to say dreams only happen when you take the initiative, what do you think I was doing for the past five years, chilling. Technically, it's my fault I can't blame anyone for telling you the truth, the reason I'm like this is because of myself. So, I need to embrace it, cause believe me I tried to change, more than five times but I failed with all that, so I'm just being me, I honestly wonder how people do it to tell the truth, what do you?

But to the person who is going to love me, if I ever have that person in the future or whatever. I'm sorry to say this but I don't think I'm going to give you 100% of my heart, cause if I do, you're going to fix it and break it again. Well, if I can, cause I'm a sucker for love ha-ha.

I'm going to give you a piece from the pieces of my heart they have broken, that I have broken, cause I'm at a point now whereby I don't want my heart to be fixed.

So, if you break it, you could break that little piece you have so I won't feel anything, turn it into ash. So, I'm sorry I'm not going to love you wholeheartedly, nor trust you with all my will, at the moment I just lost hope and do not believe in love no more. I mean, I even stopped watching romantic movies do you believe that I used to love romantic movies dude like the way especially classical ones portrayed love, that's why I still write love letters and stuff, man, the old school love, chivalry.

But I believe in being by myself now, the number of thoughts that roam in and out of my brain, if they were sold for coins believe me, I would have made a ton.

Sometimes I don't know, like currently for the past days I've been thinking and wondering. I know I've said a lot of things , made rules and regulations that I must follow throughout cause of the things that happened but if I think about it properly, yeah, I envy what other people have and not due to envy I also want to feel that certain way I felt when I had a friend when I had the so called girlfriend which I never had, just that this days it's hard for me to get that and yeah I've been trying by all means but it's not easy to tell you the truth so why should I whine about it. Okay, I've set boundaries and I've made rules that I'm no longer looking because I've been rejected multiple times without any valid conclusion whereby, I even came up with my own conclusion, that I'm weird and ugly that's why. So, I just started looking at different viewpoints, things I could be more focused on like for example, I just got another, the second opportunity to study abroad. I got or let me say I won another scholarship to further my studies in the UK, like if I feel like I want to do my master's degree I can go and do it in the UK.

So, I think I should start focusing on the positive, and no dude no. That mindset didn't get awoken by that email I received yesterday; it awoken last week just that I was sick to a point where I couldn't do anything. Like I bumped into a video which just kind of brought something back to my mind, like why be like everyone, do you think people want to be like you, do they even know how much I fucked up myself to those who want to be me. So, like instead of crying to God about things that I want I should be grateful for whatever he has given me. Even if he gives me something that I see no purpose for, the purpose will reveal itself, there's no need for me to start getting all dramatic on his face, I should be thankful for everything, big or small, even though sometimes it's hard, but I'm just glad that I got to see that now. So, whichever blessing that he hands me I'm forever grateful, spiritually, mentally, emotionally and physically, no matter what my stupid little brain thinks tomorrow, or the day after tomorrow. I'm grateful for those blessings.

Another one, like DJ Khaled always says on his tracks, you know technically these days I feel like I'm really going crazy, like honestly saying and still nothing changed I'm still grateful for the things God has given me and yet I'm still not complaining, and I don't even want to. Thats the purpose of me writing in this book just to be honest.

Basically, I'm back again to the same spot which I thought I managed to run away from this. I deleted my accounts because I keep seeing so many posts of two by two. Technically I didn't want to think about it, but I did yesterday, maybe it's because I was too tired, and a splitting headache had visited me. Or that video that I saw of the guy who his girlfriend visited him for his birthday. Lucky he is to tell the truth, and happy for him. I mean we don't even celebrate our birthdays, why am I saying we, I'm not sure you do, but I don't, I mean even my family remember after days that ooh it was my birthday ha-ha. Stupid.

But he's a lucky champ.

Besides that, I have to say these days I seem happy and it's kind of weird. Me, happy, it's weird to tell you the truth. I'm talking to people, which is a little bit considered as socializing, but it's not because of the thing of normally socializing but just because we are forced to do group work. But none other than that I wouldn't, this sudden type of happiness that I feel when I'm with them feels weird, and yes, I know I asked to be happy but not like this. Even if I'd say I'm happy every moment that I get, a chance whereby I'm all alone, I'm just going back to the dark place which I can think of eradicating.

So, the plot or twist is about to come, whereby I need to break my own heart so I can be in that sink hole for a moment, I don't want this too much of whatever it is in my life. If I want to be happy I will, with the right people, not people who are in it for seconds.

Yeah, it sounds crazy, and it is, because even myself I'm weirdly confused at the moment on like what's happening in my life, I'm sad but happy and not like those type of mixed feelings stuff, those are for people who enjoy life or something, you know those type of people jumping from one happiness to another, the ones who have too much tears in their body when they happy they cry. Dude, do you think tears of joy taste the same as tears of pain? Think about it: tears I'm used to taste like salt; I wonder if tears of joy have sugar in them, don't you think?

Anyway, listen to this, I wrote this after talking to Katie.

Note 1:

I'm afraid of the darkness, and yes, I think I've made peace with it but the more it turns out to visit me, it's more likely to want to stay.

Thats why I'm chasing after people so it may seem that I'm occupied but no, I'm just trying to tell the darkness that I do not want him to visit me in the nicest way as possible.

By letting him see myself occupied, you see the smile on my face is brought up because of joy, joy never loved me, nor liked me.

But I have a crush called sadness and she always forwarded letters my way of true love, but I never wanted to be sad, I want joy, to be happy with joy, but joy wants to feel sad sometimes, that's why she likes sadness.

So, we are stuck in a love triangle with feelings of shades

Please bear with me as I look beyond the skies

They say never depend on one to make a smile, but a smile is brought by another smile.

How could I smile alone, my smile isn't bright, but the brightness is what shines deeper inside as I try to swallow each drop of razers bit by bit.

What I mean is what I say honestly, like think about it, a mother finds happiness in marriage and kids so does the husband yet the kids find joy in friends so do pick up the phone and tell me what do you mean when you say your joy doesn't depend on other humans, humans are pathogens do believe me, we rely on others to make us happy but to tell the truth I see it, it's difficult to express so may I not be called human as my flesh differ from humans. Oh no, I'm not to speak about my skin color but the blood, eyes, feelings or emotions that show humanoid creatures features, silent, okay, silent, stay in there. My brain is not making any peace.

Just a moment with you shatters my view as I'm trying to build my own point of view. It's been said that time and patience always outshine the rest and the truth has been spoken multiple times.

It takes a lot of energy to write in this book and I haven't had the time to read every word nor check if everything makes sense and what else can it be about besides the love that I felt from deep within. But don't worry everything makes sense, it's not my first book to write.

I told and kept telling myself that I'm done with love but I guess there is this piece of me deep down that still craves it, like the day in which I just wanted to hear someone saying they love me, but it never happened, I even forgot how I went through with that day.

Falling in love but scared to lose a person for once you say those three words destruction may occur or something beautiful might, but what are the chances that something good might come out of that though?

The chances are less, that's why you turn to die in silence like how you turn you doing, if you can relate that is. In this world feelings aren't worth anything, people don't value them, what's valued is money, and beauty, those are the only things that seems to keep the world from its orbital place, for those who do not value those but seek feelings worth it don't belong here, cause a lot can be said about feelings but honestly only 2% are the ones who feel them and live with the damage every day.

Basically, the mind has a mind of its own, so does the heart. If I were to take my heart and say life is in your hands, will it enjoy a single moment or do as it desire, cause believe me they are some things that I wish I could say, but I can't cause of limitations to what's wrong and right in this world. Even my brain keeps on thinking about the impossible, I wish I could forget this world that I live in and just jump into my dreams because sometimes I do turn to believe that living in my dreams it's better than living in this world, but I can't and sometimes trying to make those dreams a reality it's quite hard, harder than anything, that's why I started saying that sometimes it's better to settle for less than the perfection of what we see in our brains every time we close our eyes, let our spirit rest in peace, with the heart beating peacefully.

It's hard, it's been days of me telling myself that I'm all good with love, like the day I was purple/blue, wishing that someone, anyone could just tell me that they love me wholeheartedly, but unfortunately, that doesn't happen much to people like me.

So guess what, my heart has been pulled from multiple sides like it's about to be torn by feelings that I possess of people who don't even look at me twice, the second look just turns to make them sick to a point where they'd just spit on the ground or maybe it's the feeling of loneliness or something. If I told you that I was in love, would you believe me, cause right now I'm denying all facts no matter how accurate or precise the results are, because I know that everything might just be in my brain, and my heart is cheering yes, yes, since it wants to be loved for the first time.

I know how I feel but with others towards me when it comes to love it's quite hard for me to read the signs, that's why I'm cooped up, and locked up all my feelings but yeah, I love her, and I wish I had someone to call a girlfriend and just mostly her.

Okay, this is the third time today writing in here, I just wanted to say this, I have feelings for her deep down I know, I could spend all eternity just by staring at her and following her everywhere like a lost puppy following its new master due to its gut feeling. Her eyes that build up peace inside my devastating heart that crumbled, and destruction is the only beauty that remains. Her outburst of laughter that scream joy when she's near to listen to the dumb words I wanted, I uttered a moment for her to catch by the ear.

Sometimes it feels like a dream I love and which I'd keep playing repeatedly on auto-replay for eternity. Her silence turns to make me want to read out her thoughts for any pathogenic thoughts that she might think, I want to kill and exterminate it so she can never feel less when she starts to look at herself, when she starts to think of life.

Sometimes I wish I could give her a warm hug, so she could feel the amount of protection my hands, heart, soul and souls heart are willing to give if she only knew. They say words can't fully express what you feel for they can turn to manipulate and turn to hurt unintentionally, that's why I wish that I could open my heart and just show her that my heart does not speak lies when it says it beats for you. Her smile and the look she makes when I turn to say something idiotic, which I may call the best thing of the day, when I turn to look at her.

The amount of freedom she gets when she sees me, but they are just feelings right, my mind is contemplating all scenes I call memories like when she said she missed me, they just feelings.

Maybe it's because I'm too lonely at this point that's why there's a lot of scratches inside this moment in this book as I'm searching for perfection as if she might ever read this, but this is for my eyes only unless I've said. So, I have fallen with feelings as big as the clouds, but hopefully they'll turn black and die on the route before something beautiful breaks, before it starts.

Okay, love, love, I don't know, one minute you're confessing your love to someone, well actually to a book and the next you're broken and what you wrote technically feels stupid to even look at. An invisible sign saying please choose me seems to be hovering above my head that's one thing for sure I know it exists. Technically I'm heartbroken because it just been laid that the is someone else and already the conversation is moving up to a whole new planet of pink love that it is as I'm in the dark but I said it though, maybe it's all just in my head, cause there's nothing in this world called falling in love with me, and it sucks much. So, I'm the friend. Everything I've ever expressed about my feelings never meant anything. This is the moment in life where I should stop caring, like I mean to force these things of illusions and face reality. I'm never going to meet whoever that person is that I'm going to fall for, even if I do, it's probably going to be too late honestly.

It's kind of boring, knowing that you have the characteristics but they are desired to be clouded by an invisible cloud which you can't see and do you want to know the irony of life, of me, is even if I start saying I'm better alone, I don't need a relationship, it's all just a lie, cause deep down dude I crave it, with all the desires God inserted in me, I need it. They are all focused on one position, because you don't know how it feels when you're the only person who seems to enjoy life alone, if you know what I mean, anyway it is what it is.

Another day again, writing thoughts, today I can't say much except that I'm depressed, or sad, I don't know, whatever happened last night doesn't sit well with me in my brain. It's kind of saying hello, I come back, but anyway, let me just start studying, study time maybe will eradicate all the thoughts I had last night maybe who knows. Confusion is one of greatest things that seems to have visited me lately, it has become my so-called closest friend. Holding a pen trying to figure out how to take my thoughts and display them as words. First all that time I spent in the study room seems like I was just wasting my time cause I'm thinking that I failed, well I did and re-wrote the exam yesterday, but it feels like it isn't working how I wanted it. So basically, there is a possibility that my semester report is going to come up with two failed modules which is stressing me out because I've never repeated a subject before, so I don't know what's going on right now. Maybe it's the reason why I feel this gloomy or maybe it's because I just woke up.

Song 1:

Maybe it's just my mind playing games

With my heart riding along in the same boat contemplating with my thoughts about the songs I listen to

Love songs to state the truth

Got me wishing to fall lately as well

Just like everybody that I see smiling

That I see holding hands walking by the route 2 by 2

One reason why I don't go outside

Second reason why I'm antisocial yet I can meet someone to talk to

Share my troubles and joys

Sometimes I'll be wishing I had someone to write this love songs too

I know they aren't perfect

Cause I'm lacking the picture painted perfect in my brain

Cause I just dream about that smile that will light up my mood

In reality I'm me with a heart that's nearly dead

Can't cry only smile to everyone who wants to utter a few words to me that's if they catch me

Cause I'll be running from corner to corner

Cause I'm tired of putting on my fake smile

That I'll be wishing mostly, someone to write these songs

These notes

Someone to hug, but they told me to be careful in what I wish

Thats why I went to specific but it's not coming that's what I see

What I feel, but lately walking it's hard no more

Silence isn't silent no more as I can hear the voice in my head talking to me loudly

So, for now

I'll just listen to music on this headphones and dream

Dream about what I want and be thankful for what I have

Note 2:

I fall in love with anyone who comes my way

I fall in love with anyone who listens to my heart

I say I fall in love with just the little attention you give

My past isn't perfect

I'm still tangled up with its strings, making it hard to forget

I never cared about love until I finally drown up

I never knew saying I was fine I was never fine

It was just my state of mind trying to hide the fact that I was lonely, a nobody

Just another ghost unable to follow the light

Searching for something called the unknown

Looking for love in every direction

Give me some attention I'm going to imagine the aisle me and you dancing

Thats when I share my heart story and you start relating to yours

Scare you away with illusions all ghosts have

A sucker for love

Became vulnerable to anyone who'd tell me that they love

I would fall no matter the stakes

Happy new year to the one whose reading this, probably nobody, it's been almost two or three days, basically three but I'm not that thrilled with it much. I still feel like the old me, the me back in 2023, why, don't know but it still sucks honestly. Just a quick reminder, don't mind the last two pages that I wrote, it's just a song that I've been working on and trying to figure out something just to keep my mind busy. I'm not an artist, I'm just a person with a pen and paper trying to figure out the patterns of my life as it is.

Can I ask you a question if I may, have you ever, or let me say, do you know the phrase, "life is like a wheel, what goes around comes around", like the good you do will always come back to you and the bad you do will always come back to you. I feel like I am at that state but I mostly would say that I seem to be tangled with the strings of the past, they are kind of dragging me when I try to push forward or my mind is sharply focused but I'm on a road filled with people, but I'm blind, I keep running to different people or if you believe in reincarnation I'd say my past self must have committed suicide and I'm left with the stains and scars to try to heal.

Trust me, all the explanations I've got in my tiny brain don't make no sense at all, and I just found out that all the girls I've tried dating with ended up wanting to be friends, how twisted is that weird is a word people use but they aren't aware of half of it.

I think I've had my take for 2024. Can we skip to 2025, maybe that fresh start might look better if I take a glimpse at it while looking at it from here, kidding. I want to say I don't believe in the future but someone said what you see in the future or what you Invision is what you can have but will never show you how to get there so that you can appreciate the moment, and a dream is a vision as well, even though they say some dreams aren't always going to shine, but they will fall in the darkness of the heart, the core of the heart that is.

So I've had my take of it, the past three days of 2024, were filled with disappointment, boredom, anger and irritation, if I turn to imagine happiness I'd say it was when my emotional dependence was being feed, even though my heart was there my brain had nothing to say but end it and go to bed, stop talking it's not worth it, mind, I was trying and still trying to get rid of this emotional dependence which will lead me to another level of this loneliness further than I am at the moment, so basically I'm in a ring as the referee watching if my brain or my heart can defeat the other and gain the championship to do whatever it pleases with I.

So, can I turn to ask you a question mostly if you are a guy if you're reading this, and tell me if you can relate, lady you're welcome to participate as well. My situation has been long, about 4 years now and 5 years of being single, and 2024, it will be 6 years in November. So, have you ever, like for you dude have you ever had feelings for someone and no matter what you do, you couldn't remove them from your heart, you ignored them, moved on to someone else, again and again, get yourself heartbroken, but they are still there as pure as a diamond, sparkling in the destruction of your heart, and once you tell yourself that you know what, I'm tired of this feeling, I'm going to tell them, or bump into a stupid video which says it's either now or never or a song that says tell her how you feel cause you might never get the chance to do it, and that stupid heart of yours agrees, you take your legs with you and approach the girl and she tells you this;

"So, Dimpho, Dimpho, you better listen to me like, thoroughly so, Dimpho Rampedi, I don't know how to put this ay, but then me and you, we will never even ever date, we will never date me and you, you have to give up dude it's been so long for you trying to get me to be with you, you've been trying and you can see it's becoming difficult even you are just trying but you no longer have the strength so you have to admit that SpongeBob doesn't want me, why are you making this a big deal, why can't you just pass from it instead of making things complicated, me and you will never date, I don't know how to explain this how like, I don't know it's like I wish I could scrape out myself to pieces and explain this to you, so please, I'm begging you,

please, and it's not because of the fact that I have a boyfriend or whatever cause even if I break up with my current boyfriend I'm going to move on to someone else, I'm not going to come and say I'm going to date you no, No! you see. I don't want to give you too much stress were you'd be thinking about me, or whatever, on your academics, that's why I didn't want me and you to continue chatting, I was avoiding this, I was avoiding this, your putting pressure on yourself and you can even see for yourself that it's not working, like just move on dude, we move on as people even if we get hurt we move on, so who do you think you are, you can't move on, for a period of years, years! like wow Dimpho dude. I don't know how to explain it but me and you will never date, if I had an interest in you, we could've dated so there are gents who wanted me for 3 years and they gave up so who do you think you are, you have to give up man, just give up, cause nothing will happen between me and you, so don't hope that I'm still chatting with SpongeBob that means me and her can plan out something, no, not at all, like that won't happen, it will never even in hell happen just move on with your life, focus on your academics, and delete everything of mine in your phone, so you will never even see me, you will only see me on WhatsApp when I've posted that's all"

The message goes on but some of things can be written in English with my heart still dangling on my ribs, I had to translate that, but it pains more in my language than in English include the tone of expression, well that what I was told and I almost, almost just to state this, almost cried, my eyes were watery so I quickly grabbed my headphones and listened to music as my eyes dried up, have ever felt that pain.

Lady I don't believe that a guy has ever said this to a lady, never rejected a girl like this, if you like a guy they'll never tell you that they have a girlfriend or whatever, they will accept you due to the fact that they want to sleep with you not because they are in love, that's why you most of the time they get heartbroken by them assholes, so that pain of being heartbroken by them, didn't match this one, I'm sorry if you feel offended but I said it, and I'm not taking it back.

If not, congratulations to you pretty boy, but if you did, that is one of the reasons why love is kind of shitty, sorry but it must be said. Now I am friends with her not because of revenge or something, but I'm still friends with her because I care about her. Yep, I am a simp, don't know even what it means I just saw a video of a guy washing dishes while his girlfriend was on the bed taking the video, this day's people are fucked up. The language is becoming too much now is the truth. So nice guys like us turn to die inside quickly and quietly so. We are able to carry the pain of ours and the pain of others who we care about and die in silence. The worst part is that we turn to be rooted in places where we see that the person who we care about doesn't really care about us.

We are just their insurance even though they don't pay anything to make sure they covered, another state of mind or the truth if you are a girl you can test out this theory, ask a guy best friend if he'd ever had feelings for you before you became friends, there's a chance that he might lie, but if you know him well enough you can tell that the person is lying or do one of those pranks or lie detector test, but most guys or guy friends are your friends because they really like you and care about you but couldn't get the chance to tell you that's why they decided to be your friends to be there for you and care for you because they love you.

Believe it or not it's your choice, truth is always cruel to those who see beneath it.

Letter: *Yara*

I wish I could just say it's a state of the mind, the way we meet it was ideal like a scenario, a scenic view. The last memory of you, I promise just to keep in these songs and to carve your name on my heart as you'll always be my spiderGwen.

I remember the first time we meet with you telling lies with me following away, we were high until we both broke the lie and started talking and enjoying every moment, talking about your favorite movies and music, got my heart hanging about your favorite hero's and villains, telling me that Iron Men is your favorite, how kind he his and smart, for what he did in the Endgame movie. Telling you that mine was Spiderman (Miles Morales), then you started calling me spiderman. Which kind of made you my SpiderGwen.

You started smiling and blushing telling me you'll be Gwendelyn, then you sent me a video I made the theme to the song I wrote, so when you listen to it and watch it, you'll think of me the same way I'll be thinking of you. We started hanging out a lot, late night texts, late night drawing competitions, late night contests, we used to make until I asked what's your favorite thing after music and movies, then you said," you are for me the thing after movies and music".

It was kind of a sweet move, I wasn't expecting that, within it became a thing the love between Miles and Gwen, me, and you, but the saddest thing about us being them was that Gwen always leaves in all the spiderman movies, but we never cared. We started talking a lot, sleeping with my phone in my hand realizing in the morning, you telling me to wake up, to not fall asleep yet, you do the same, teaching me Arabic, those are the last memories I'm writing and preserving in tune. Hoping that one day we might collide again, I never thought I could meet another me in this world, but lord showed me there are more like me.

I just wished he could have kept you and this, I'm not bullying you, I'm just stating the truth.

I miss you.

To my Spidergwen
Yara.

So basically I'm back at the same spot again, see moments ago or should I say days ago I was busy in my thoughts thinking about Yara a girl I meet online and we kind of connected, so says the songs I wrote and I actually missed her because love it or not she was the best thing that happened to me back in 2023, and I kind of missed her more than anything cause she was just like me, excluding the sad depressed stuff, and it came to my realization that I worthied her.

Moments later it was Pearl, whereby I went out of line, me and her used to have this bond before each one of us decided to take separate thoughts, the worst part about it was that she forgot everything we used to be. Unfortunately, she is now a lesbian according to her, but I still feel like that girl I meet is still in there somewhere just that the world has been cruel to her to a point were she decided to change her own identity, and it worried me.

We were in a call moments ago not moments but days ago but I'm still bothered by it. The secrets we used to share from both sides are barricaded by a force unknown, I tried talking to her but it's strange as if like I'm something or someone she doesn't recognize or maybe it's the whole change thing of being a lesbian, and me not being comfortable. I choose the truth between lying to her and pretending, due to the car accident, the scares left must have caused her to overlook some factors and made her less himself I don't know, she no longer wears skirts afraid of what boys or the person she will date might think. Cause frankly speaking the scars weren't good looking.

Maybe that's why she decided to change gender cause with girls it's going to be different, the worst part is that when I told her about that she no longer wanted to respond , and added on, saying what my mother has told me, that the new generation doesn't understand anything, the reason why we have those kind of genders like lesbian and gay it's because back then there were people who had a different sex organ different from their physique. Like a man who had the sexual reproductive organ of a women and a woman who had that of a man.

In their home language they used to call them "Tona kasadi", it really didn't have nothing to do with feelings and such, sleeping with someone and not feeling them doesn't mean you were supposed to be a man and the other way around, it just means your spirit doesn't want to be with that person, your spirit doesn't feel connected.

So basically your sleeping with the wrong person, and unfortunately, after saying all of that, the conversation took a toll, and it was meet by silence, the only thing I got was "I hear you" and that was it, and she dropped the call, and it took me to a point were I realized that I should keep somethings to myself. Therefore, I went to the app to apologize for overstepping and from there the conversation stopped, making her one of the people I used to like.

It took three days of pain my heart beating hard and not knowing why is it this heavy, beating so painful, guilty off course I am, off course I felt so, so I decided that day never to talk or say anything that I think of basically nor share what I've been taught, and for this to happen she always told me she's old and needs her family members to stop treating her as a kid. Grown-ups talk, no matter what the conversation says to you no matter how it will hurt you, it's a conversation where both parties have to indulge each other with facts, opinions etc.

Regardless of ones emotions not a debate, but she only listened and let it get to her head, still now I apologize and still believe that maybe I'm tired, just tired. After the conversation with her I've been thinking to myself that, maybe it's time whereby I let the darkness, loneliness and depression take over cause what's the point, it's always the fact that everything, every time when I say something that's always going to happen. Which made me realize that from now on she isn't going to talk to me no matter what, while still on that note, sitting alone and listening to my thoughts as the music plays in the background, I got a text from my ex friend, Katie. Which states that she missed her friend, and I honestly didn't know what to type and say remembering the fact that the history that we have sucks.

Her text must have meant something, maybe that she's in need of someone to talk to, she's going through something, she needs someone to count on and honestly when I needed someone she was never there, she has people or friends that can be there for her I just don't know why she decided to choose me back, why she texted me and the worst part is that if I choose to fix everything, she's going to do the same thing again.

I mean I'm going to do the same thing again, be there for her up until she feels better than leave and never look back again. I mean even a doctor is visited from time to time for consultations not only when you're sick and me I turn to help when it's my turn to seek help from her, she was busy, I text her she takes about weeks to respond, so is it ideal for me to count on to someone like that.

And it's not like saying just help her of fix that relationship, I'm actually tired because we talked about this twice, and I felt like I was forcing things, I stopped talking to her and gave her the choice of being with those she values, and guess what she wanted to talk, like again, fix things, I was tired, and I'm still tired because she's not the only person who does this, there are multiple even SpongeBob. So why should we, I mean even in a relationship when a person keeps doing the same thing over and over again, and you sit that person down and talk to her, and talk to her, and talk to her, and talk to her, forgive her multiples times you turn to get tired.

Did she change, I don't know and I honestly don't want to know, hopefully to the next friend it will be better than how it was with me cause for me, at the moment I'm still deciding if whether I need friends or not, I'm tired, that's why I say I've made the door only to open on the inside only, so that the friends that are inside my circle can open it freely and leave the circle, but since you can't open it outside to get in, that's where you'll remain.

I'm just trying to put myself first these days, and it's actually lonely and depressing to have no one to talk to, not have anyone at all, worst part is to envy others, when you see a group of people laughing together enjoying every moment a couple laughing joyfully, you turn to envy them, it's hard but I'll try to manage it.

Pain is virtue, that's what they say right.

The worst part about me right now is that I'm losing interest to the things that I used to do, like writing poems, lyrics, making music and drawing. Like this is funny, if you think about, do you know how desperate I was to find a friend worst part a girlfriend, because that's the only thing that was revolving in my brain, because a true girlfriend will always be there for you, talk to you from time to time, care about how you feel, like a girlfriend sums up everything that I required, everything that I needed. I went to dating websites to multiple dating sites to a point were I realized that all websites are the same, likes are important, followers are what people care about, and some girls just want you to flirt with them like remind them their pretty and other stuff but not caring about what you're interested in like a long term relationship.

Unfortunately, I never found what I was looking for so here I am again, in the new year. Technically, I'm not expecting anything new or a slight change this year because I've been living my life like this for as long as I can remember, nothing new happens, it's always the same thing repeatedly. It's just reality that is.

Question again.

Is it more prideful to want to be alone, enjoy your company or drown in your own sadness than to associate yourself with people? Technically being alone will cause you to do everything alone even seeking help becomes hard but is it prideful to be by yourself and not associate with others.

Thats what it's believed to be, that's what they think, it's not protecting your own peace of mind and dealing with some of your own issues by yourself. So am I being prideful to feel like I need only me alone, and create a door which you can only push from the inside in order to get out, but letting you inside becomes kind of hard, basically in other words it becomes impossible, that's what it will be called as days go by and nights turn to a summers morning.

So, I am trying to brace myself for what's to come, cause a lot is coming over this year, more than I can handle but, with the will I got a way will be forged so. I've got nothing else to say from here on out, besides state my thoughts that keep patronizing me but, I'm grateful for them, because they make me a part of me. They sometimes turn to remove the pain that I have and introduce something like a little spark, even if I'm lacking the words to brighten up the darkness that keeps on getting darker and darker.

But hopefully one day I will find it, the spark in the woods, that will light up my insides I suppose even though that's the problem. I don't want to hope nor more, I don't want to do that cause I'm tired of it all, so first thing. I want to build this project and see if I can make a business and grow from it, and basically see what happens, so without further no say I bid you adieu.

If she was a dream, would you follow her, or maybe stay behind because you know what lies at the edges of the so called feelings. If she was a dream, would you choose to stay asleep for eternity or will you be awaken because you know the outcomes of eternal slumber with a vision set on her. Hi, so here I am, back again to writing, basically this is going to the most confusing thing to read since I don't put out dates for when I'm writing, I used to do it, in the first Notebook but hack, it's not important to know the dates like Einstein said, time is relative so basically I had to check conversations but nobody is texting and I keep on checking every minute to see if I got something, and yes I did text first, what do you expect I always do that no questions asked, and reply fast.

Anyway, that's not important cause I managed to take my headphones and pump some music and write in this Notebook. Basically, I'm asking myself this question, what are feelings? And why do I turn to have them? I get that feelings are used to express a certain mood you're feeling in order to understand your emotions, but why does it have to be involved with love or searching for someone, why do we feel a certain way when we see someone and start day dreaming it back it's all insane. Why can we just dance like birds in order express feeling to show love I mean that's simple and straight forward, no one gets hurt ha-ha.

One of the most insane thoughts I have to say, basically is not a thought but something I've done which is creepy, have you ever stared deep in your eyes before, and try to look what's inside of you, and I mean it not figuratively but realistically speaking. Standing in front of a mirror and looked at yourself for a moment and try to ask yourself basic questions like who are you, what are you, where do you belong. Don't do those creepy things in horror movies, heed. I hate horror movies, that's why I don't even like going out at night.

Sometimes it gets confusing cause you turn to get lost in your thoughts for a moment and start shedding tears from your beautiful eyes. It's weird, but I once asked myself while looking at me in the mirror, how life is in the other side of the mirror. Is it the same as how I'm living it right now or different? I even thought that maybe the other side is different, but our minds turn to click with the same thought when we start saying let me go look at the mirror if my hair is done well or dressed appropriately. Some hypothesis roaming around.

Hey, again, I need to stop greeting as if someone is actually going read but I wrote it anyway, I'm writing another song at the moment, I don't know what the title is going to be cause it's kind of hard to put it in tune like, I've written the words down and I have the beat with me, but it's hard to work on something beautiful while you're having a bad day or something like days I guess. Basically, the song goes to SpongeBob, but I'm not going to tell her anything because we aren't talking, it has that little moment, were she was still like smiling for me, you know. I like that part, but I don't know maybe I'm crazy, or that's what I just missed so far in life. Cause I found this old letter that I once written for her, back in the days when we still understood each other, when we were still trying to figure out if I can eventually be the thing or something like nothing. And I wrote this;

"SpongeBob, call me dump, stupid or crazy but I still don't get how my system works dude. I still miss you and yah I know that we've never dated so be cool alright but I still miss those conversations we held and nope you aren't the first girl I've ever liked for me to do all this shit but you're the first girl that my soul has ever stared too deep and felt of leaving my body just to meet your spirit.

I tried removing you out, but this shit is like chess when you're thinking you are going to win then you lose, I don't know if you get me or what but still my inner Dimpho still got that crush for you, I am not better or perfect but the perfect canvas I see it's when I'm in it with you.

At first I felt no need to compete with a dude to see who wins the goddess Bee so I gave up, the second, I thought me and you it's oil and water but clearly we were both in liquid phase but now even though I'm tired as fuck but the will is still there telling me to keep going, the weirdest part is that sometimes I picture you blushing cause damn your smile has got me feeling crazy it's like that smile that keeps the whole solar system all together without it the wouldn't be life and I am not doing this to please someone but I'm doing it to please my souls heart even if it were for 2 seconds I wouldn't mind or love to break.

I don't care those are the rules of it we falling in love forgetting the distance, the distance your falling till your actually broken but I don't mind it with you, I just wanted to feel what being loved by you will feel like, wanted to know your hug, see your smile close, how you'd stare in my eyes while lost in thoughts, how you would pronounce those big three words to me.

Bee SpongeBob
From Joker_Dimpho"

Basically I wrote that, and it's not what I was, it actually happened during that time where there was this other guy trying his shot on her, and she telling me she just saw him smiling and couldn't help it, basically

I'm ugly just to tell you the truth based on her point of view. The desperation on what I wrote though, is it being desperate or being heartbroken like, "please don't break up with me, I'll do anything please" type of thing, weird but I have to say my writing wasn't that bad, it was pretty dope though the metaphors, the stupidity and idiot in it shows common nonsense like I was having a headache. Kidding it's nice but I think I could've done better and made it sound less broken and in distress and yes less desperate. Good thing is, I never sent it or else I was going to wear a diaper till now.

But basically yeah, I read that and listened to her voice notes from back then like way back then and just thought I should make another boring song about falling in love with her. This is what I came up with.

Song: 2

I still say, roses are red, violets are blue
In a room full of art, I'll still stare at you
From my eyes to my brain to my heart to my souls to my souls heart
Never before had I wanted to say so much but said little of my own heart
felt so much but stayed silent
Cause I'm tongue tired
I don't see you in the moon and stars, that's what dreamers do
I see reflections in my eyes, on every little thing I do
And your eyes stole my heart
Your smile gave me life
Your presence made me high with the touch that left me breathless
So, it beats for you, it breaks for you, it loves for you, it aches for you, and
only you
You got my heart spinning in a loop
As you painted colors on my heart like the sky blue
They say to make something special you got to believe it's special
Thats why I believe in us.

I basically quoted 60% of the lines from other different poems I don't know how many, but I quoted that's why I think it's impossible to make, I don't feel what I wrote for it on the first verse that's why I stopped and listening to music is my only way of expressing. You know, just to state something, I don't know if I've said this before, or what, but during the moment when it was me and her basically me choosing to be her friend cause I couldn't be apart from her she told me that the guy was her long time crush, she started liking the guy ever since she was in matric and stuff but it's in the past anyway but I have to make this song but only the first verse and the title it's going to be Souls heart, iconic and beautiful, now I just got to ask Amanda if she could help me out with a chorus, even though I highly doubt that she will help me cause of our history.

But there's no harm in trying right, so basically I've made a lot of songs now I think I'm going to put them on YouTube cause I keep losing some of the songs that I made, sucks, I'm happy that I lost them cause they suck big time, but I still feel like they are important cause they remind me how bad to good or okay I came to making music but will see.

Sometimes I turn to forget how awesome the thing called imagination can be, like smiling alone is sometimes crazy too, like I don't know it's just weird to have an imagination at this age, I think. Like if you'd choose in anyway how your life would be like, in a movie which movie would you choose?

I would be stuck in-between choosing The Fault in Our Stars and Spiderman Across the Spider verse. They are pretty iconic and the way the love is in there, it's pretty nice, now it's just a thought, that came while I was listening to music, and unfortunately, I couldn't stop smiling about the what if, the possibility of removing all things that are against fantasies and just imagine that. So basically, I wrote about this, but I lost the first Notebook that has all the information so I'm just going to give a brief overview of this thing. To those I left on the mountain's peak, here is the way down, even though it's boring to write about the same thing repeatedly. Everything starts with a question my fellow reader as you noticed.

Have you ever loved someone to a point were that person breaks your heart and the little bones that your heart has, ripped, the same very veins in that heart which it uses to give you life, and turn to say that's it, I'm done with love, I'm done with this person. I want to move on and you remove that person out of your life, and every little thing that reminds you of him or her, and once you're on the route to life, you turn to find someone new, someone different and turn to say, "I like that person", genuinely so.

And remember that you forgot about that person who broke you up to pieces. With that new person you talk and talk mostly in my part, you talk partially because you'll never be the only fisherman in the lake, you'll always find a bunch of people fishing at the same spot you're fishing. So, when you talk to that person, emotions escalate drastically and weirdly like that. Then it never works in my case, or it works in your case, and you turn to realize that she is similar to that one who broke your inner inside.

Not like 10% alike, a little bit, nope, like around 70, 80 % exactly the same, the way she is when comparing her to the first one you fell for. Thats the history, after getting hurt, or maybe I was over exaggerating or something, I don't know, but when SpongeBob decided to choose another guy over me to date I was just at the moment were I felt like ripping my heart out and honestly, a guy expressing his feelings, pulling all stunts in the romantic or play book or whatever book it's called and a guy just comes along with a fucken smile and looks at her, already she's in love.

I mean, a smile over things you did to prove to her and shit that dude I really am into you, are worth nothing to a stupid smile, worst part after distancing yourself from them they start blaming you saying it's your fault, they needed you, and you weren't there, while they already choose someone over you, what do you expect, huh, what do you expect, to be the third wheel, to be a doctor, I only fix never get fixed.

By the way, do doctors go to other doctors when they are sick, or they just prescribe the antibiotics for themself, if so that's awesome if not that's a waste, cause here in my country traditional doctors can't heal themselves they have to go to other doctors to get healed if sick.

Girls are fucked up basically, so after taking time away from her, blocking her and stuff, I started talking to my history, which was a part called moving on, and she also choose another guy cause he's handsome and smart and all that. Like I said to my mom, on a date, the hole conversation is supposed to revolve around the girl, cause if you as a guy, talking about yourself it's called eww, like not a turn on or whatever, as a guy you talk about yourself when asked, straight to the point, simple and clear answer or add a little joke in it. But don't talk about yourself too much, you're a gentleman, like 20% for the guy and 80% for the girl.

Getting to know each other, still the same thing, nothing changes, if you talk about yourself your regarded as boring. Like the example above, she loved his smile, and already head over hills, so if no intentions are shown by the guy that he truly wants you and just lets you blah blah about himself, do you think it's ideal to date that person.

What I like to called it, is commenting, the girl talks about the first love and it's time for me to say something about first love, it's going to be a short statement, if you watch romantic movies, you know what I am talking about. A date is never a 50/50 conversation, where even the guys love says, "I just like listening to you talk", that's crap but we still do it in life, adding comments. I have a lot of examples but I'm not going to go into detail about, because you know what I'm talking about, validation.

When the guy starts acting up, doing stupid things, or in some extend abuse, the lady turn to say he wasn't like this when I first meet him, like really, you liked the guy cause he's handsome, he's got that bad guy attitude, you said you wanted sleepless nights sometimes, regardless on that. Focus on this, did you ask him about himself, anything, not ask him to comment, but personally let him blah blah about himself for once, no, no you didn't. Cause most of the time we turn to focus on the future and the now, ambitions, dreams, family, see himself, and the other stuff, never about the before, and I get it honestly. You normally find them in the middle of a relationship, which are sometimes hard to handle. To others who feel offended and such extremes have happened, my deepest apologies from my hearts core.

Some advice; as women learn to respect yourself, don't be controlled by the dialogue set with illusions your eye seems to aid.

I once had this conversation with my class colleague, which I stated that if I go out with a girl on a date, I'm going to ask her about her body count, to some it's going to be offensive, but to others it's a giveaway, you know me partially now, that maybe I'm insecure, or I'm not good in bed, or I've never tried anything like that and etc. Honestly, I'm just saying, please don't get offended. But to continue...

I realized that she was exactly like SpongeBob, both loved natural hair, dressed like a lady, down to earth girls, smart, beautiful smile, illusional laugh, majestic eyes, personality kind hearted but dramatic like that of SpongeBob, just that she never had to hide his dramatic side.

Thats when I decided to kill my heart and go back, and my heart now is neither dead nor alive, it's just there, confused like it's owner. I don't know why love can't be like in the movie Elementals, where two different people can try rather than just to judge you know, come up with their reasons why it will never work. But love is for those who look beautiful and rich and whatever things I left out.

So basically, that's the summary of my past, the history I had with Amanda and without the details. The moral of the story it's I'll never be chosen no matter how much I prove to people how worthy I am to be chosen, I mean I can choose myself cause the isn't no guy who could do what I do to prove myself, and if there's one, they are just lonely and depressed like me, or life turned downside up for them, not upside down.

But if you got something, it's not because of what you did, it's because of what they tired of and want to settle, they are tired of bouncing from one place to another, they had their fun, their last option is you. Underline last option. Thats why you're with the person your dating, you only know his ex, only, not his or her ex's, if you knew them, trust me, you would ask yourself questions like how did it end on you. Your basically, I'm just saying to make myself feel better, and trust me I'm smiling right now as I'm writing this but trust me, it's just how things are in this life dude.

Technically speaking, when parents say you're not old enough to be in love, or is it love it's not for kids, whatever it is, it actually means that finding it, and keeping it, it's hard, that's a route which you're going to walk barefoot while walking on a route filled with broken glass, snakes, scorpions, and all horrible things you can imagine, if it's not with you, the skeletons are always well hidden.

Sometimes I forget that I'm that nothing in people; I don't know why I keep forgetting that. I actually asked her if she could be of assistance in helping me to write a song, more accurately to state, a chorus only, and she said that she'll look into it when she arrives home, and that was 3 days ago, I sent the rough draft of the mixdown including my verse, all she had to do was listen and write, record and sent. Thats it, and it's basically going to be that thing were you all would say she's busy, she isn't home, like really, I used to do that, give reason for everything they'd do but it's not going to work, cause she's posting, going through media since the past 3 days. So I did what's best for me, deleted the messages and the rough draft cause what's the point right, the main thing was to say no, I mean I get it, it's going to hurt, but it's better to say it, than make me wait for the rain in the dry season you know.

Saying it's coming, it's coming, up until when exactly, when is it going to arrive hey. With the other thought, half my brain is trying to figure out, I'm a little bit awful at the moment not liking what I am, as I feel empty and that person doesn't even care, I mean I know you can relate because we used to talk about these things dude, but since the little distance she be treating me like a total stranger, and during that distance I was the one trying by all means to try to reach out to her, while she was moving on, I think, I don't know but just I'm just a scrap yard now. I've downloaded 13 comedy movies to try and neutralize the feeling I seem to be having with laughter and joy. But after watching one movie it's back to the same place again. I honestly feel like I need a dog. Maybe a wolf, plus their over protective it will just be me and my wolf man or something.

I can't make music no more, or maybe I should say I can but the will for making music in me is actually dead, I've been working on a song to express feelings for Pearl, but it seems hard, I don't know. I'm even asking myself how even, since when, I have beats multiple beats and I can create this perfect version of a song in my head but to put it down in a paper is a little bit hard. So, I'm starting to ask myself if my heart is dead.

If you've had this thing were by you turn to look at somebodies picture for a while, stare at it with your heart beating with your mind blank like you were put in a spell to not move that's what I kind of see. Or maybe my feelings are dead or my heart, I'll be glad either way, catching feelings for a person is a lot of work, and I suggested that maybe I should write it in here but I forgot it cause I was busy working on a new book, but if I remember it, I'll be sure to write and yes it's super important I guess basically. Remember when I was talking about how this year will be different, well yes, I basically think it will but to my surprise she's back, Yara is back actually, and I think I'm happy, I think I am, cause my inside are feeling weird like someone is tickling me, weird.

Love Note: Pearl

Every note that turns to be noted becomes one of the utmost important things in daily affirmation

Just like the first days when you take notice of the stars when stargazing

While constellations tell tales of love through the Milky Way

A sight more significant eyes turn to blister from its beauty

It's one o'clock

Writing a note to the duchess precious pearl

I do apologize for I am anachronism

A state which I believe the roman era black knight could have been I

I told I that writing emotions will no longer appeal

But in my hand a pen that seems not to stop inking for the lub dub sounds have been silent for drastically the ghost of I might be working for acknowledgement

Truth be told change has occurred

For you had to

After all, how could you stay the same when every interaction with you reshaped a part of me

Hard to explain, but somewhere along the line, without realizing it, you gave me a piece of my heart

I hung onto every word, every laugh, every moment, we shared

Thinking maybe just maybe there was something more

Or maybe the thoughts I had, there wasn't

It was a one-sided dream and now,

I'm left wondering were these moments as meaningless for you as they've become painful to me

Before the change

But lately I've been thinking, and maybe it's time to take a step back and say let them lose me

I just wished I could've told how I felt about you

Every time we talked there was a voice inside me hoping for something more

I wish our conversations, deep conversations could have hinted at feelings beyond just friendship.

But hopefully we are, and were just two people passing through each other's lives, destined to teach one another a lesson rather stay forever

I'll keep moving on, love you stranger

From Dimpho

Note 3:

When did I suddenly love the rain so much
Summer was joyful and memories were sunny
People were smiling, and love was floating in the breeze
Suddenly rain seems to be owning my heart
The wet grass and paddles bring faded memories of age back
The peace of drops landing on your face
The sounds of drops landing on the floor
The breeze, the one and only breeze
That brings you back to life
It's a world of fantasy willing to get lost in
The grass has never been greener
So as the leaf's on the trees
My breathe has never been clear so as my spirit

Note 4:

I want to fall in love
 I want to fall in love with you
 Not the love envisioned in every blink of an eye
 Perfection is what the canvas states
 Unfortunately, art is made with perfection like the thoughts of I and you
 Fall like the way the stars fell for darkness
 Blessing sad lost souls with joy as they twinkle and twinkle up in the heavenly skies
 How they give us hope in every smile of a shooting star to believe in love
 I want to fall to feel the pain kuekuatsheu feels when crying for the moon
 Lonely as they drift more and more apart

Note 5: SpongeBob

I still want to love you

Love you like the stars and moon up in the heavenly skies turning darkness into beauty

Nightmares into constellations that live to tell tales of fantasy of...

The first sight set on scene to bear witness of

Love you unbelievably, so tales of us turn mythically passed from generation to generation

For the brain and shovel buried the heart 6ft under but still sounded the drums of lub dub

Unburied then buried 12 ft under now the lub dub causes earthquakes when calling your name

I still want to love you

But no words uttered say meaning of my souls heart

Carrying roses, lilies, daisy's, azaleas in both hands awaiting your soul to give to yours but

Slowly they decay

Without losing no hope but excitement

Adrenaline keeps rushing through the souls heart

A thousand notes written day by day

No perfect rhyme approaches to match the crystal eyes fallen for

Poems written before the night tucks to bed but no perfect stanza to match her beauty

Long wished upon shooting stars on buried cries and whispers

But a ghost is I no sign can be seen nor felt besides floating around to catch a glimpse of the sunrise

During moments of spring

Joy approaches countenance

I still want to love you

A wish only remains

To the stars twinkling above the sky, send me a shotting star to know your secret
So, I can twinkle bright
With the love I have for Her

Note 6:

Question?

Do birds ever fall in love like humans do?

Do they love with their hearts, soul, or spirit?

How is it that when any animal finds the one to share a life with just immediately knows?

Do harming birds harm their sweet melodies to say humans have found love?

Maybe they harm to express their feelings towards their lover

Do tweeting birds ever fight over love when their sounds fall on the ground beneath the tree roots

Do they ever tell lies like "I'll love you till forever" or "I'll always be there for you"

Does the flower know that bee's don't love them

For every single visit Mr. Bee makes to Mis Roses Red he always leaves with pollen to give to his queen

Does the beautiful Mis Roses Red know that she's being used

Or is it all just the circle of life

Do animals ever act out of love like humans

How do they know that they found the one?

The one to spend eternity with in just a flicker of an eye

Do they ever get heartbroken?

Cry for days while trying to catch every tear with memories adding salt and pepper on the broken heart

Do they remember their ex, meaning those who they dated

Do they get a sharp pain every time they see them smiling after a few days of breaking up

Do they spent sleepless nights too when they don't want to dream about them

Is that the reason why they just fly in one place for a moment while riding the wind

Blowing their tears away
Or is it just the circle of life

How do they get the courage to show their love and still get turned down
over and over again
Do they ever get sick of being heartbroken
Do they say "I love you" as if it's a game the same way we humans do
Is their love for real?
For it's beautiful to have love like that
Pure love still exists on this big world
Or maybe it's the circle of life

Note 7:

Can we exchange bodies
  Maybe I'd feel better if you do and even you might
  A lot of people told me a life without friends is the best life
  Life alone is peaceful
  But how peaceful is it with your thoughts always shouting, talking negatively, envying those who said those words to but do not abide by them
  How does this lonely void get filled up by the peaceful life of being alone
  I envy those a lot
  They told me you can have friends and still feel lonely and want to be alone
  Can we swap bodies so you can be alone and with your friends
  For I've tried to fill up this deep dark void with music, drawings, singing, poetry, but it's never filled
  So, I lost taste now
  I'm embarking on reading novels to get lost in a different world that will make me delighted of wearing the stars under the moon
  Instead of lying while awake in the belly of the night overthinking
  So can we swap bodies
  You become me and I you

Hi, I'm guessing your still reading this book, but I think this is the part where I should thank you for engaging with my thoughts or feelings, or drama as some might say. I know it's not much, nor interesting but I sometimes feel like this notebook and the person reading it, like you, and others who had can relate. At this moment it's been weeks and months since I wrote my thoughts and my troubles here, I guess this is the point where I have to say this, I really don't know if I'm depressed, or whatever. I don't know what it looks like, but loneliness is a big thing that revolving in my blood right now. I sometimes even like to say that I think I'm overexaggerating this, it's just a stage you know it'll pass.

And basically I know I've written a lot of things in here like the people who played a part in my life for the moment, mostly girls but I think most of the information it's about SpongeBob, and I know you must be tired of hearing about her, and honestly I am too, I guess it mostly moves around her, but honestly I just have to say, it's not about getting over her, maybe about how I loved her and still do.

But I must show you something reader before I continue with today's writing, the cloud following me, and it's about her. I found this notes I wrote to her but never got the chance to show to her, because appreciation for literature in some other creatures is not part of life. Some I just wrote not for her, but just thinking, bored, lonely, but I hope you keep reading for we are nearing the end, but I don't know if it's an interest for you or not. But I think this is something that plays an important role in I.

Here are the notes written.

Note 8: SpongeBob

I wish I could tell you that I miss you

But unfortunately, I can't cause you'll use the same word to describe me
"stupid" that is

It's just painful that you never saw my love for you blossom like a flower

And over protective like thorns of a rose

A mistake is what you saw

As days turn to nights and nights turn to tomorrow

I try by all means to forget about you

The memories I had with you, still held, and still worthied

As I tried to toss away but a little piece of you remained like a stain

A stain on a shirt unseen but felt with a little bit or aroma

I can't believe, I believed and lived a dream with you as my love

But found out that you're my illusion like the stories and notes I write
that make no sense

I still stay awake through the night trying to recall the dreams back with
my soul holding flowers of roses waiting for your soul to come back

But as time keeps ticking a flower peddle falls down as if I'm playing,
she loves me, she loves me not

The roses in my soul are decaying slowly as I've been waiting

And my souls heart is tired of telling me to move on, but my brain and
heart keeps denying and reminding me about the past memories

While I want to look into the future

From time to time, I told you

I can't give you my heart as it has scares and bruises with names of
people carved on it stating they were here to mark their history on my heart

But I can give you my soul's heart as that only God protects and it's hard
to break

I value you with my souls heart but if you ever feel like that's too much

I can give you my heart too
So, you can love, break and carve your name on it, just like everybody else

Forever it remains as flowers in the hands of my soul

Note 9:

Can I say that I want to fall in love
Just like the way my peers are in love with their partners
I don't really know what people who fall or are in love do most of the time
But I want to feel like them
But maybe it's just my ultra ego being needy
Or maybe it's just my soul wanting to have someone to communicate with the same way I do to myself
Care about me the same way I would to her
So, I want to fall in love
But it seems that I can't fall in love though
Maybe my soulmate died while trying to find me
Or the traffic to come here to my heart seems to be too much
She might be stuck on the way
I wonder if she listens to my heart talking
Or if we ever dreamt of the same thing
I've been waiting and searching for so long I'm beginning to lose hope a little
Maybe not a little but too much as I'm starting to be falling in love with the skeletons I've hidden in the closet
Will you lose hope if I did, and will you consider to make me believe in love again
Cause I'm starting to build a flag pole so long that the whole hold can see and place a white flag for I surrender
My heart is smashed to pieces
Are you as equally heartbroken as I
Or you were never searching as you knew you yourself was made for I and I alone
So will meet in the future for now your relaxed
As time will tell as our destinies intertwine

Well, my heart isn't looking good to tell you the truth
Cause I've spent most of my entire time looking for you
Did somethings and still do things that are shameful of just so I can find
you

*I need you to be my medicine because I seem to be getting weaker and
weaker by a day
With my heart no longer beating the same as it normally should
Will you resurrect me from the dead when I stop loving or leave us for
dead so
Scavengers can pick the remains of my love as souvenirs
I apologies to you for future reference
For I've went from person to person thinking it's you and I got broken
If I never show love and affection to you
Just know that I will always love you
And thank you for finding me in this big dark maze of a world
For now, I just hope you'll keep me forever and ever
You're not to blame for what I am
The blame is on me
But I hope you can help me become a better person
The person God has made for you
X.O.X.O*

Note 10:

I want to fall

I want to fall in love too

I don't know if I really do

Or maybe it's because of the fact that everyone that I know is taken

I mean not taken but, in a relationship,

And every time when I'm bored, I wish to talk to some of my friend but unfortunately

The time they have can only be taken by their girlfriends and boyfriends

Maybe it's because the time I spent with my other two friends loneliness and darkness is causing a little bit of distress to me

Eruption of volcanos that causes destruction inside I

I want to be with someone at least to know that I exist

Not call me or text me whenever they need something

Someone who won't wait for me to tell them that I'm not feeling well

But rather check on me not because its mandatory as I'm human

But because of the fact that they care about my well-being same way I do about them

Maybe I need love because I envy the smiles that my friends have when they talk about them

The dreamy eyes they own when they are talking to them instead of talking to the walls and ceilings and the insane person in my head

From time to time, I said I'm done and over with love

But it gets harder by the day as my feet turn to point to the door and my breath seeking fresh air

I try to focus on something else but removing the hole love things from my own brain

It's hard to stop and runaway from love as it doesn't need you but want you to witness it while it gives itself to others

Dying slowly

Note 11:

I have to state this before my heart implode
I miss you stranger
It's weird how two strangers can turn to have a bond as if they were born
as twins
But I'm not going to state a love note cause all of them suck
So, I miss you
Like the way I see people in hijabs I turn to envision you
Thinking it's you
Cause it's you without you no you is precious enough like the smile you
have

Note 12:

Infinity, they say love will last
Sorry it's just a thought I can't suppress
What is love, for I feel certain headaches when I turn to think about it
Which leads to a heartache
Only wanting to sleep, rest my soul as it has been seeking for as long as I can remember
Chest pains of rejection always appeared
I always tried to numb the pain with sad songs
Sometimes asking myself in the mirror how life is in the other side
While sometimes I'd like to think that I'm just being all dramatic
Yesterday I got a visit from my friend loneliness, and he asked me if we could chill
Unfortunately, I said yes, for I needed some company
We spent hours listening to music and watching the Big Bang Theory while eating until darkness started knocking on the door
I let him in too and we all laid on the bed expressing our thoughts while starring at the ceiling
As we kept talking my thoughts gained nails with my heart feeling its under pressure
But I couldn't tell them anything because loneliness might strike around saying that it wants me to feel better
And darkness might never think of leaving too
So, I set through the night
A hangout turned to a sleepover
Loneliness took my heart as a place to fall asleep
And darkness decided to take the hole room and cover me with his body filled with nightmares
I took the bed and tried to close my eyes
But no hallucinations of dreams that I loved came
So, I just stayed while awake through the night

Like a night light for my two friends
While I hate

Note 13: SpongeBob

In two minutes, I fell again

Fell in love with a heart that wasn't seeking but I also wasn't

I thought I was over and done with love trying to remove my emotional dependence from them but I'm back again

Lonely and the only thing that I think about its how she'd call every time she felt lonely

When she was with others the thought of her was always in my mind but mine in hers was never a visited only through the lonely night

That night the moment will

Tonight

Yesterday and the day before yesterday I was sited alone as usual

My brain wanted to talk to me, but I didn't want to listen to it complain about how it's always right

So, I interrupted it with a load of music of sad songs I listen too

Truth of the matter I fall fast, that's why I fell so fast to one single word she said

I loved how she made me feel like I existed, like I'm a human too

But nobody stays for long, but the promise should be just left alone or kept as may once my heart make promises

My brain always figures a way to fulfil them

Listening is one of the hardest thing a human can do, but not me, I've always been there to land an ear for those who want to talk those who want someone to just listen, but the favor never returned. Or maybe it's my fault for not sharing, reader I fall in love with attention I think, when someone gives me attention, I turn to overdose my thoughts cause that's all I want, just to be noticed. From a young age I never had no one to play with or hangout with, do sleep overs or enjoyable things when I was a kid, but back then I never thought of it as being lonely.

And believe I tried making friends, my best friend or ex best friend was my neighbor, but he was never allowed to play with me, I grew up watching movies and cartoons to move past that with raging feelings so not to mention how I was treated by them when I went to play with him. From primary school to high school which struck me when one guy was singing the song Lonely by Akon.

That I really had no one but a TV filled with many cartoons to watch or anime as some may call it. I had a girlfriend though, in the 11th grade, lasted about a week, but it's understandable, the whole lonely stuff was too much weighing in my brain that's why I don't even like calling her my ex nor anything, because I never dated her.

When I first moved to University I was introduced to SpongeBob, an iconic girl, I thought, and I still think she is. By introduced I don't mean formally so, but she was my step nieces friend and we talked for hours and hours, she gave me attention. She gave me attention, made me as if I am human, noticed me for the first time in my life I had someone who looked forward or I looked forward to talking to her every day, and with feelings, she made me care about her, not my intention to fall for her, but something happened which made care about.

She gave me attention unlike no one else in this world, someone I was willing to open up to. Maybe that's one of the reasons why her name is filled up in here more than any other. I stopped talking to her since 6th of May and today its 21st of June, and we always called each other every week and stuff, talking for hours like two love birds experiencing love for the first time in their life but to tell you the truth even on the 6th of May I didn't feel like I was talking to her.

I stopped talking to SpongeBob, the real SpongeBob last year, this year she actually disappeared from my life to be exact. She found new people in life to replace me, and technically you all know I was head over heels for her no matter how badly she fucked up my feelings. But I valued her, for the past days I dreamt of people, and I don't mean it in a poetic sense type of way, but I've dreamt of Pearl and Nikky, and she called me on the 4th of June, 21:56 p.m. to be exact.

She was lying in bed, wearing her light pink hoodie, and her first question was why aren't you calling me anymore? As if I don't know, tell me if I'm a culprit for being in a place where I'm being needed than were I'm not. My lonely self-called brain wanted me, loneliness wanted to accompany me, and she didn't want to do that because I'm nothing right. So, what should have I done, I told her that I was busy writing an exam tomorrow. The reality of it is that, everything came after her, I always made her my first priority. I was never busy to talk to her, just like last year. I was willing to drop everything for her, because I enjoyed every moment that we spent talking, but in my brain, she only called me because the people who she normally hangup my phone for didn't entertain her that day and she called me, she called me only because she was bored or feeling lonely.

When I first saw this, like I was talking to her, she said she must go to bed, hang up the phone, just to talk to someone else. We aren't dating, but what happened to the SpongeBob who used to say hey, there's an incoming call I have to answer, and after this I'm thinking of heading to bed talk later. What happened to that person? What happened?

I was the last option, the bottom of the barrel, when there's no one else to talk to her, the last resort was me, I guess, and she just said ooh good luck then. I guess that's the part I wanted to say, I feel way too lonely now, was it the correct thing to do, cause sometimes I imagine getting a call from someone or a visit were me and that person can talk for hours, what do you do when your eagerd to just talk to someone, anyone. If you are me, you would try by all means to accompany yourself with these novels in front of me and try to engage yourself with them, take your headphones and burst the volume up and listen to sad music to a point were you would not even hear a knock on the door, possibly the will never be a knock on the door, just to state the truth.

Question.

Do you realize that males in referring to all male species, we also have feelings too. I mean men, boys, males we also have feelings, we cry the same way women do, feel pain the same way women, there's not much difference in-between the two of us. But we have to be hard like a rock all the time, but you turn to forget that a rock does also lose its strength in due time and can be melted. It becomes soft as sand. But that's not persevered in this world, men will always be culprits of all the crimes because it's our nature as believed, the nature portrait upon us by women.

I get the fact that men turn to do a lot of things wrong, but it doesn't mean all of them are, the same way we talk about women. I was watching some videos on Instagram and I bumped into this other video from a doorbell video recorder or whatever name they call it and this girl just budged in crying, not just the normal cry, like the cry that touches something deep inside, like the cry of a baby in pain and she fell down while her other friend was trying to pick her up to comfort her, the words "why me" came out breathless and almost made a drop of tear fall from my face. My eyes were filled with water, but I just couldn't let myself cry, but I felt what she felt. It's one of those thing which I was talking about in past like commenting on dates and stuff.

I used to tell myself that I should work on myself, and forget about girls, treat them the same way I've been rejected, not care about them, laugh at their pain as they are the ones who give much more pain to us or gave to me. But for now, I think in-between a million, there's still a few who still got their hearts intact. A few pages back, I might have said that I'd like SpongeBob to break my heart to so many pieces so that I can be toxic, not sure if this Notebook or the last, but I said so just like the way every girl that falls for toxic guys. But I've always been the guy who is old school, I still believe in buying flowers, picnic dates, reading dates, poetry notes, writing letters and even slow dancing. I still believe is show love don't talk it.

Talk is cheap, rather show, but I guess in this generation, everything changed or I'm the last one who still believes in action speaks louder than word. Why do even girls choose people who they can't rely on and choose us good guys to be the ones there for them? Honestly if you're a women please answer this question so I can understand why.

Reader today is the 12th and I have to say I miss her, or miss talking to her, I guess. What's your advice or take on this? I know it's weird how topics on this book switch left, right, front, and center, someone once told me that I should seek therapy, to talk about things that I can't express to people or in this notebook. I honestly think I'm on the edge, like I am at that point where I'm losing who I am completely. Am I or have I, at this turn were there's only one memory to completely forget who Dimpho is. But I honestly missed talking to her, just that I'm not what's called noticed wherever.

Should I give it a last chance or start to fix it, or just let it go?

As I did what my blinded heart instructed, its official, the blame is on me as usually, because I'm always talking about school as if she doesn't or the course, she does isn't important just because it doesn't require you to prepare for exams, her words not mine. Yes, I've complained about school work, group assignment and, to think of it, that's all I've ever complained about. Never have I ever judged a course nor the course she is doing because people do different things due to loving, so who am I to judge?

I learned that lesson during my 11th grade in my English class. Madam Pasha would always say if you think your smart, keep it to yourself, and turn to look at me with the tiger eye, that sent shock waves down my spinal cord, during my departure at high school, she was the one giving us our certificates, and told me to remember those words, to remember every word that the teaches have taught me. Not school based words, but the words they used to shape me, never forget where I come from. I'm not perfect, I do judge but most of my time I keep it to myself, cause I'm not better than anyone, never. When I told her that I have said a lot about school and postponed our video call, I always called back, and I did reader, I did dude.

But she said maybe she's crazy then and that she thought losing her would be better for me, cause she's exhausting, what can I say about that, she is really hard headed, she is.

Someone even once said we are like mom and dad trying to avoid divorce but it's the only way out.

Well, my dear reader, I have to say this is were I stop with the notebook, me and her haven't talked since, thank you for engaging with my thoughts, a note to say my byes for now.

Note 14:

She told me she loves

I smiled my head telling my heart that she's bluffing

I took a deep stare in her eyes, and I saw her blue iris moving with the beat of her heart

With disbelief I asked

You love me

Nervously, she stated yes, with a blush looking down

My brain trying to analyze and calculate a perfect way to explain this as a prank

My heart breaking bit by bit as my lungs deny it the breath to breath the feelings that are spread by her in the atmosphere

Impossible the brain of I tries to think itself

How could one love him that carries me

He who looks like he's living life backwards while its forward

My heart was breaking

As I denied it love countless times for a person like me isn't worth anyone's love

Impossible are the words that came out

Why me, were the ones that followed

I don't know she said

Being around you just brings a different feeling in me that I've been trying to ignore for so long

But my hearts been beating the sound of drums for this feeling

It punched a hole in one of my lungs and broken the ribs to try and find this feeling

And it did, it's from you

I turn to look on the ground

Smile

And the lung breaths in the feelings so my heart can drown in them

Let my brain rest from the nights spent thinking about the perfect love while I never found it
As I look up, she was gone
Turn to look sideways it was pitch black

Close my eyes and open the again
It was just a dream

I thank you and welcome you to Uncapped Feelings, were the seed was first planted.
Falling in love with a lesbian.

Don't miss out!

Visit the website below and you can sign up to receive emails whenever T.Charles Rampedi publishes a new book. There's no charge and no obligation.

https://books2read.com/r/B-A-MEQTB-SIKRD

BOOKS 2 READ

Connecting independent readers to independent writers.